Cascade method

Created by Tara Boykin

This book belongs to

Halloween Fun!

INDEX

Trick or Treating Ghosts

Moderato

Sca - ry ghosts are / What if they come   *float-ing up and / to our door say,*   *down the / "Trick or*   *street / Treat?"*

prepare L.H.

Knock! Knock! They   *go,*   *"O - pen the door,*

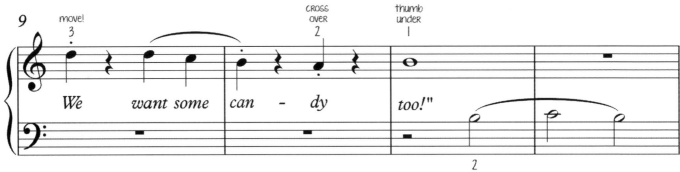

We want some   *can - dy*   *too!"*

Teacher Duet (student plays an octave higher)

Moderato

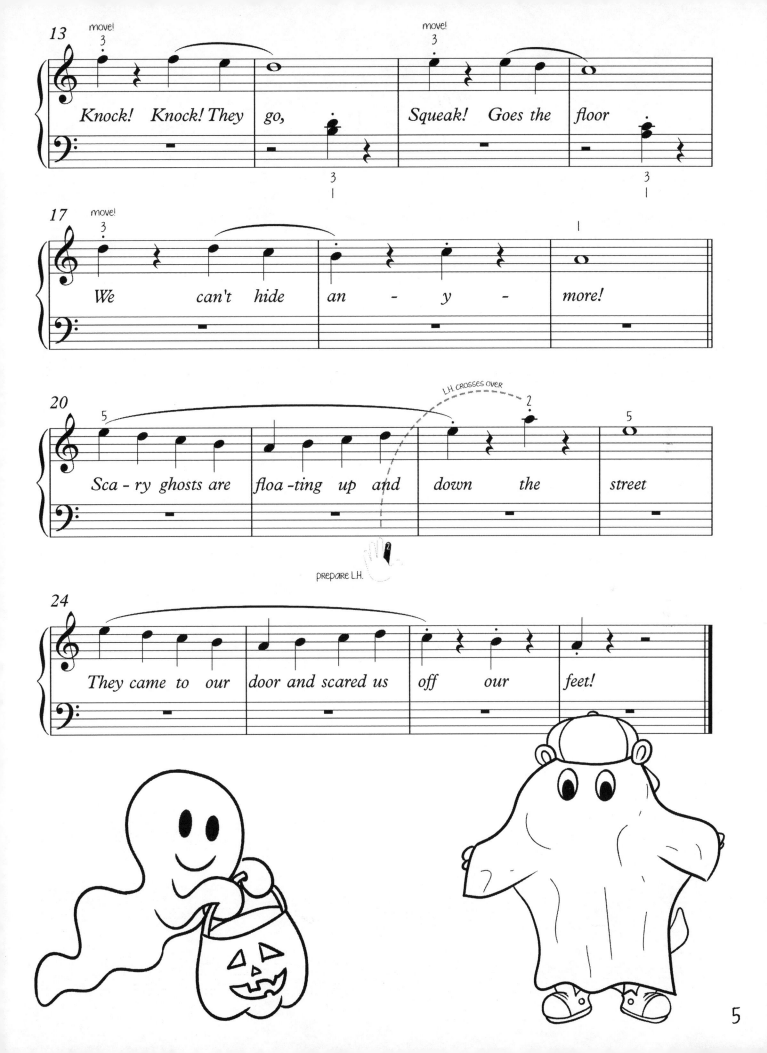

Skeleton Waltz

Teacher Duet (Student plays 1 octave higher)

Moody Magic Potion

Graveyard Monsters

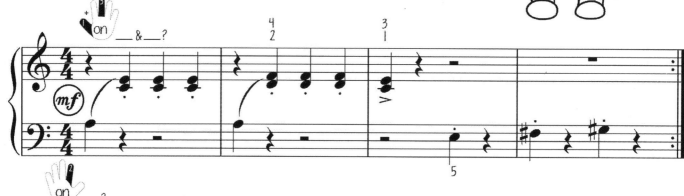

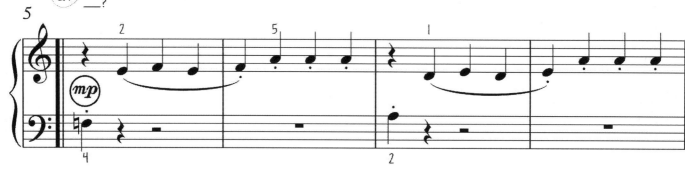

Teacher Duet (student plays an octave higher)

10

move! 2

move! 2

1.   **2.**

Repeat everything an octave higher   Play both hands an octave higher

Dracula's Sonata

Moderato

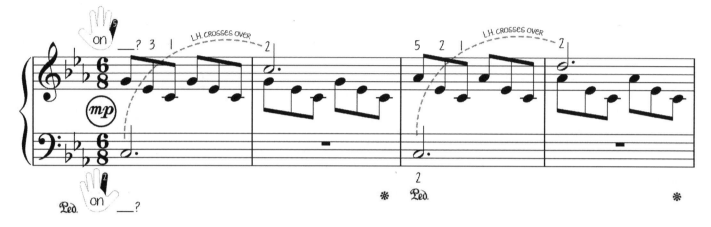

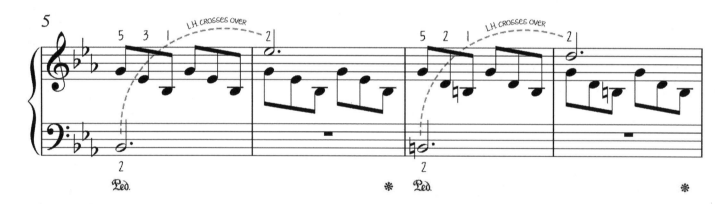

Teacher's Duet (Student plays an octave higher)

Moderato

repeat everything an octave higher   Play as written

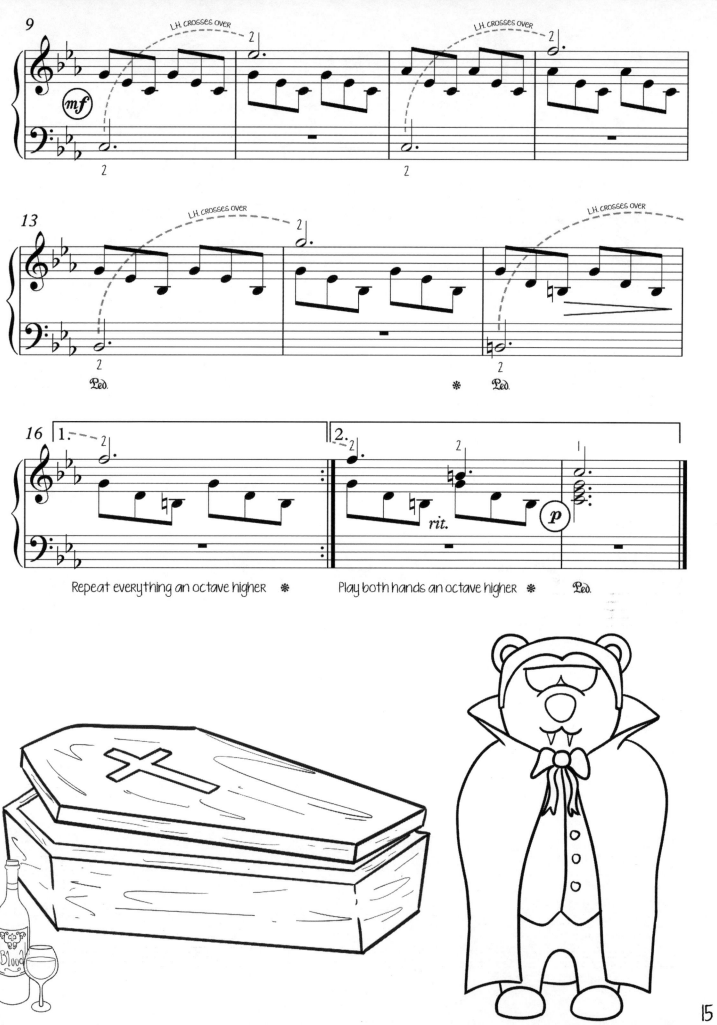

Repeat everything an octave higher ✸   Play both hands an octave higher ✸   Ped.

Colluding Cats

Presto *Play in a swing rhythm!*

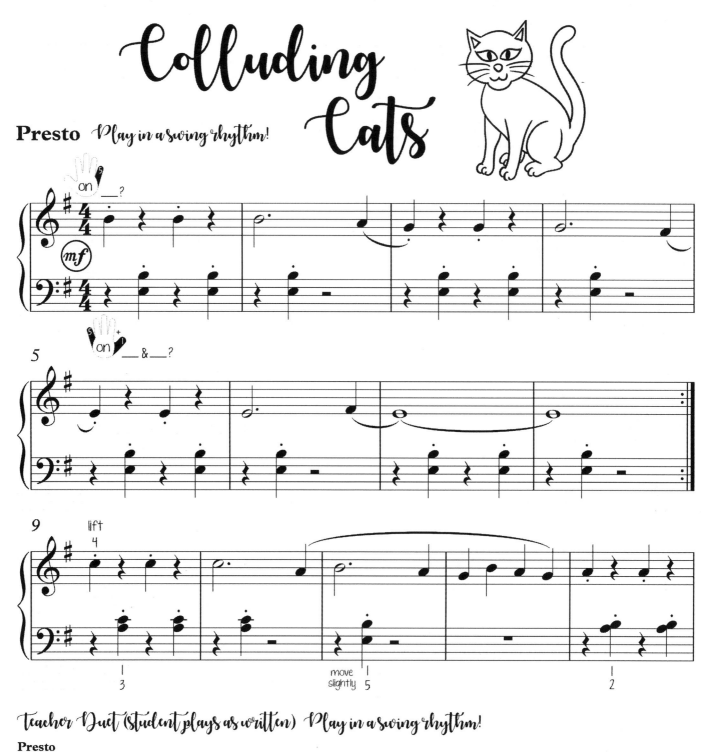

Teacher Duet (student plays as written) *Play in a swing rhythm!*

Presto

Repeat 3 times and fade away... Ending after 3 repeats

Get softer with every repeat *p*

Under a Witch's Spell

19

Misbehaving Bats

Teacher Duet (Student plays an octave higher)

Creepy Crawly Spiders

Presto

Teacher Duet (student plays an octave higher)

Presto

Repeat everything
an octave higher

Play both hands an octave higher

Cascade Method Certificate

Congratulations

to

_____

for finishing

Halloween Fun!

Teacher: .... **Date:** ....

Made in the USA
Monee, IL
15 September 2022

13982674R00015